QUANTITIES/DAMAGES

Books by Richard Howard

QUANTITIES/DAMAGES
Early Poems

Richard Howard

Wesleyan University Press
MIDDLETOWN, CONNECTICUT

This volume is a collection of poems previously published by Wesleyan
University Press in the two books *Quantities*, copyright © 1962
by Richard Howard, and *The Damages*, copyright © 1967 by Richard
Howard.

Some of the poems in *Quantities* have been published in *Hudson Review,
Paris Review, Partisan Review, Poetry*, and *The Second Coming*. "The
Return from Montauk" was originally printed in *The New Yorker*.
Grateful acknowledgments are due to the editors of these publications
for permission to reprint material that first appeared in their pages.

Some of the poems in *Damages* originally appeared in *Circle Review,
Craft Horizons, For Now, Quarterly Review of Literature*, and *Tri-
Quarterly*. "Bonnard: A Novel," "A Far Cry After a Close Call," and
"Private Drive" part ii (there titled "The Landscape Garden") were first
printed in *The New Yorker*. "Crepuscular," "The Difference," "Secular
Games," and "209 Canal" were originally published in *Poetry*.

All inquiries and permissions requests should be addressed to the Pub-
lisher, Wesleyan University Press, 110 Mt. Vernon Street, Middletown,
Connecticut 06457.

Distributed by Harper & Row Publishers, Keystone Industrial Park,
Scranton, Pennsylvania 18512.

Library of Congress Cataloging in Publication Data
Howard, Richard, 1929–
Quantities, Damages
    1. Howard, Richard, 1929–   . Damages. 1984.
  ii. Title: Quantities.   iii. Title: Damages.
PS3558.0882Q3   1984   811'.54   83-23304
ISBN 0-8195-5105-8 (alk. paper)
ISBN 0-8195-6094-4 (pbk.: alk. paper)

Manufactured in the United States of America

Wesleyan Poetry

First Edition

Contents

DAMAGES

I

QUANTITIES

To Anne and John Hollander
The mind uncertain of its meat
The heart's law in dispute

Advice from the Cocoon

This leaf, delivered to your empty hand,
Is crumpled like a letter from the fall:
Unfold it gently, it is legible
If you are patient with mortality.
Perhaps it bears a message for your loss

Among its broken veins. Here is a grub
Of summer, modest in its public state
But growing by a private appetite
To prouder life. If property is theft
As Proudhon claimed, the proof is in his jaws—

A larceny of leaves. What grub can own
Grub eats, and eats away the rest to weave
A serviceable shroud against the cold.
The larva, not quite wool, but not yet will,
Is wrapped up well between his other lives.

Would you, like him, survive at any cost?
Then seal yourself in layers of yourself,
Warm as a worm, until there is enough
To eat your heart away and still have left
Enough for the hungriest winter and beyond.

Jubilary Ode on the Hundredth Anniversary of the Birth of Marlene Dietrich

And even after hours
Of waking and a little sleep,
When you by impulse walk
Abroad some natural morning
Or immoderate night,
So fondly will the earth adjust
Its formal longitudes
To fit your stride; so freely will
The light consent to fall
In with your way of looking at
The world; so willingly
Water itself run up to your
Dry mouth (as for dear life)
When you would drink: it is as if
You slept through every one
Of all the ages requisite
To raise the bright trapeze
Of blood within your body, hang
Your acrobatic eyes
From the still unruined arches
That chamber in your skull.

Like love in Shelley, moving with
The easy unconcern
Of its own motion, the purpose
Of your overpowered
Self lives upon itself, and each
Excess of separate
Feature balks some other of its
Singular growth by a
Kind of general song. There is
An innocence in such

4

Accord, a music I can hear
    Beyond our carnival
And all its obstreperous cries.
    Simple to tell by your
Breathing, by your heart's meters, that
    You are no accomplice
(The record makes it clear—you were
    Erroneously charged)
In our crime of being Somewhere
    The night of Anytime.

Beyond the emblems of your state—
    This corkscrew crossed upon
Its like within a looking glass—
    I see only a blank
Ground without shadows, as one of
    Flat gold: the heraldic
Heaven without a star in it.
    For if there should be stars
What constellation could they cut
    Upon that abstract air—
What zodiacal beast assume
    The rigor of your pose?
Exhibit X in the endless
    Alphabet of our loss,
You find yourself on the unsworn
    But unperjurable
Witness stand of life: not merely
    Overripe or raw, no
Longer hiding out, like us, but
    In your undistracted
Flesh and fabulous bones At Home.

And as I watch you living in
    Your skin like birds that take
The accustomed air of summer
    With no evident need
Or care, it is a cool comfort
    I derive from noting
How for your amusement (always
    At our expense) the best
Seats in the house have been reserved
    For you ahead of Time.

At Compo Beach

Drastic in its claims upon
Our two-dimensioned holiday
Where sea and sky so neatly hinge,

Your body standing in the sun
Becomes a site of sudden change,
Accuses where we would applaud,

And criticizes every hour
Of light with shadows adequate
To prove the flattened air a fraud.

You walk across the stony beach,
Appropriately negligent
Of effort, and in spite of each

Inhuman task I summon up
To justify men being here,
Facility, I see, is all:

Where one tall bather is enough
To be our season's Centaur, just
By wading slowly out to where

The sea's green fur begins at length
To grow against you, and your own
Accustomed skin gives way to end

In a flourish of salt, swart hair.
How well the unsaddled ocean serves
As stallion half to the human beast!

And for the time we idly stare,
You leave Connecticut behind
With an obsolete shirt and socks and us

On shore—to join the heroes you
Have never heard of in the sea,
Irrelevant as any myth

To all our merely human loves.

Petition

Teach us, please, appropriate movements, drill
the hard declensions like a grammar, broken word by word
until at last we grow into the speech
You have granted. Trivial Venus, help us, for we come
unsuited to the custom of our blood
and the other juices. Extenuate our carelessness
especially now, when promise of green
weather rends the lymph: show us a way wholly to mend.
    Mourn
with us for the lost teddy bear; collect
the serpent and the unmentionable duck from our bath,
and restore the doll banished whenever
we cried at parties or would not say Thank You. Intercede
for us: we shall lose our hair. Comfort us
with stomachs: we shall be unhappy. Accord something more
than a useful failure, discover in
us the habit of your moving Law: send us from ourselves.
Possess, Lady, for we are every one
sealed in the envelope You give. O Goddess, intervene!

From the Remains of Count C. W.: after Rilke

It was in Karnak. We had ridden out,
Helene and I, after a hurried dinner.
The guide reined in: Avenue of Sphinxes,
Obelisk—oh, I never felt so much

a member of the moon's world! (Can you be growing
in me, Greatness? You were too much for me
Even then!) Is travel—search? Then this was a find.
The watchman at the entrance gave us the first

clue to the startling scale. How silly he looked
beneath the unchecked self-assertiveness
of the gate. And now, to last out our lives,
the pillars—take that one! Wasn't it enough?

Ruin excused what would have been too high
for the highest roof. It stood and held up
Egypt and night. The following fellaheen,
luckily, hung back. We needed time

to put up with this, it was almost a blow
that such a *stance* could still be part
of the being we die in. If I had a son
I'd send him here (when it comes time to learn

things that have to be true for yourself):
"There it is, Charles. Walk past the Pylon,
turn and look . . ."
                              Why doesn't it help *us* more?

That we could bear it at all was something
—a lot—for the two of us, you looking ghostly

in your linen duster, silent, ailing,
and I very much of the hermit in my theory.

Still, the mercy of it! Remember the pond
with the obsidian cats sitting around it,
monuments—to What? Presences, then,
and so committed to that magic square

that if five, on one side, hadn't been knocked
over (weren't you flabbergasted too?)
they would have held their Court just as they were—
feline, stony, mute. Everything here

was judgment. Excommunicated pond,
the giant Scarab perched on its rim,
and along the walls the epic boastfulness
of kings: Judgment. And yet at the same time

Reprieve—who would have believed it? As figure
after figure took the clear moonlight,
the carving, every outline accurately
hollowed by shadows to a kind of trough,

became a Vessel, held and yet withheld
what was never witnessed, never hidden:
it, the Secret, so secret in being there was
—needed to be—nothing secretive about it!

The books just leaf past it; no one reads
anything so obvious in a book
(what use is it, looking for a name):
the Unmeasurable forced into the measure

of sacrifice. Just look: what is Possession
until it has learned to give itself away?
Tout passe—things. Help things on their way
and keep your own life from leaking out

some crack or other. Always be the giver.
Herds of asses, humpback bullocks, crowd
to the place where the image—King's, God's—
childlike receives and smiles. His sanctity

is never out of breath. He takes and takes
yet lenity is his law, and often will
the Princess merely clasp the papyrus bloom
instead of snapping the stalk. *Here* all

sacrificial ways abruptly end,
the Sabbath begins, uncomprehended by
the long weeks. Here man and beast
drag off gains the God knows nothing of.

Business is business, and may be,
however high the interest, profitable;
we try and try (the earth can be procured)
but giving only price, give up the prize.

Saturday Morning

Beds are made close to a wall
    flat
Against the blank places.
This is so that most faces
Can turn away from all
    that.

If I turn, the time swarms.
    Word
Of mouth carries the message
Up and down the soft passage
From a hive that hums
    hard.

I am not lonely here:
    fear
Dissolves in mirrors, some
Dangers melt like sweet salve
On a wound. You must have
    come.

Rumors of Real Estate

He speaks of a white room showing
Barest at night, shadowed only
By the lamp under which his cat,
White as well, warms in a brightness
Of refusals. Of course there are
Imperfections, but until now
He has been able to shut them
Up or away, into darkness
Behind the blank of his white doors.

Naturally we all suspect
Some other sort of chamber where
He works his living out, warden
Of an implicating space: not
Only purple with unexplained
Obscurities, but gathering
All time in images of dim
Insistences. A various
Room, and full of forms, reflections.

But the truth is down a long hall
And in another place. Here are
Cruel colors, terrible cold
And a burning quite as extreme.
On the changeable bed someone
Else is lying and lying quite
Miserably. Now, following
Trials of temperature, come
Tests on teeth, examination

Nail by broken nail, and nightly
Obligation to employ each
Bright instrument that hangs upon

Its hook. This is a right surround,
Binding blur to brutality—
The genuine decor. How pat
Our word *apartment* falls in here,
For this is the life he divides
From the others, a death apart.

Natural History

What since August, when the sound
Of bees filled the lindens
And broke like a hot
Berry rotten
In ripeness
Where we
Lay,
What
After
Late motions
Of the sun, what
Grief on the hills, what
Chill stiffening the stream
Changes our love thus to our loss?

We have outgrown the weather;
The months have made only
Diminishing days.
Questioning, we
Were eager,
And grave,
But
Now,
Given
Our wan tact
And the wasting
Of fevers, who could
Hope to print Hell's lavish
Product on a face of snow?

I do not know how we fell,
Having once embellished
Every bud with bloom;
Yet if sap runs
At the root
Of time,
Down
Where
The dark
And warm life
Hides away, then
May we grow again,
Re-according by light
The heart of our green season.

The Old Men Playing Boccie
on Leroy Street

A sense of Fall without the trees
That make their rot so decorous,
A lot of ashes in the air
Tasting oddly of surrender—
This is the place, appropriate
For such unsightly men as these,
Dispossessed and almost holy,
Almost depraved, playing games
Against each other for the long
Chances of a little gain
This afternoon upon the clay.

The river hauls its burdens down,
Lapping greedily like doubt
Between the banks of ashes. Here
They are playing, the mad ruined tribe:
Ignorant, not innocent, and yet
So terribly sure of who they are.
For them it must be difficult
Believing in death, at least before
The sunset, when the opportune light
Hangs like a victim so long in the sky
That all reminders of the dark are dumb.

The old men play until I think
Their laughter is the bravest sport
I ever listened to in nature;
For if their triumph gathers out
Of what is merely argument
To us, the very ground on which
They play is merely graves to them.
Ask of their broken faces, How

Do you savor life? Do you enjoy?
And as one mouth each scar will answer,
Crying, 'I appreciate pain.'

Listen to their voices, words
Echoing over the gritty court:
Something has been given up
But they are playing. While I stand
And watch their game, the western clouds
Accumulate and the world turns back
Into its empty sky, judging
Not as the judge judges, but as
The failing light decides, falling
At last with the exhausted sun
In shadows round a helpless thing.

L'Invitation au Voyage

Wandering with you the shore
That parallels our river
    Like a second thought.
Singular and sad I wore
The habit of a lover
    Almost inside out.

Night in its black behaving
Muffled every lamp and dyed
    The wooly season,
Pig-iron boats were leaving
For the lake, slowly the loud
    Bridges had risen:

A landscape for the lonely
Or the lewd, as you observed,
    When of a sudden
Something steep and with only
Momentary warning moved
    Out of the hidden

Harbor. It was a dark boat
And *Cytherea* it said
    Low on the long bow.
"A cabin for two," cried out
A voice, and I saw a head
    That I thought I knew—

"Fifteen days to the Island:
We sail tonight with the tide!"
    I remember now,
Turning, how your face went blind.

The river sighed in its bed
    And although a few

Gulls were loud in their abuse
You did not once look up. When
    To their obloquy
No protest was made, I chose
To learn what I've always known:
    We shall never go.

Hairy

Here is a roughened instance
　　for distrust
Growing upon me, a sense
　　of reversed
Intentions, something exposed
　　that should lie
Hid, but flourishes ever
　　as summer's
Ripest weed. It is an old
　　problem, how
To divide the truthfully
　　bare from the
Barely true—all surfaces
　　are something
Of a paradox, whether
　　cumbered like
Mine with this irrelevant
　　camouflage
Or naked as your own. Which
　　approaches
The honesty of bone? I know
　　one answer
Only, for myself. The hair
　　that darkens
On my simple skin informs
　　the round skull
And my red desiring heart
　　with the same
Black fur: this ragged edge and
　　lunatic
Fringe are all the body bears
　　to show of
A gaining outer darkness.

Five Poems for Pierre de Ronsard

I   ÉLOGE DE GLAUCE À SCYLLE, NIMPHE DANSANTE

Eyelids flicker to create
Flame upon her cheek.
Phosphors palpitate
As I speak

And the lady is lifted
By a darker dancer;
Quick and explicit, as if in answer,
Ardor has shifted

Flesh, deployed the bone—
So would she discommode
The body to bright stone
Alive: a line, a node

Until before me as I stayed
A salamander careless played
And lay and shrank not from the fire:
'Tis Venus' worm, and represents desire.

II   TU ES SAVANTE, DOULCE ET VERTUEUSE

Gather up the growth of day
Dressed in summer, silk and scent,
        Indolent lady.

Gray and blue veils slide away:
Are you the greenest continent,
        Tropical lady?

Ripe the human colors lay
Where she fell impenitent,
        Declining lady.

Lounging maples will arrange
Our fall: the greenest hinge

Of summer once undone, there is
A god no longer in the weather's house.

Have we not seen how maples, red
Or leaking gold as if they bled,

Swung on their spindles, slackened,
Spun and fell in cadence likened

To a bright and blurred chorale,
Comic colors at a festival?

IV   RESSEMBLANCES DANS UNE GROTTE

How easy, in the cavern, where we lay
Dividing lavish senses into clay

And darkness, to extemporize a world.
The crusted shells, for instance, curled

Around the iridescence of their cause—
Were they not likenesses, a soft applause

Of matter at its own sure imagery
Collected in that cavern where we lay?

Imagine the bivalves there (whose slippery ears
Were seemings of our own), some pink and clear

Or pale as any further flesh of yours,
And others reddened as if from the source

Of cordial rhythms in a qualm of cold:
Such were our semblances, the oyster world

Of lovers in a quiet place; yet one
Sweet mollusc in the clammy cave, upon

Comparison . . .
                        comparisons are dumb.

V   LES DEUX AMANTS DESSOUS LE VENT D'AUTOMNE

"Chaos of Archaic Change": a garden
And a garden faun, ingloriously streaked
Or else beneath the lindens cracked
By saturated leaves, the burden

Of a dropping season and a gray—
Prophesying, I should say, a bitter
Sequel to the old weeks' weather
And our burning time of day:

Leaves and hours will fail together,
Ruined on the bright pond water.

At Bluebeard's Castle

Water is sour, the air is lonely here
And all the noises of this natural shire
From stable or from sty are not enough:
The ear has memories of its own and will
Not drown. I think you'd better give it up—
Question the local gentry. Go away.

Perhaps I *have* a certain chamber, one
That has no walls. The light is modified
Only by the bodies of my guests
Orderly hung, in solace for their time,
Their fever and their loss. Do not become
Another; it is dark already here.

I was glad when they came at first, every day
Moving among the animals like kin:
We would be happy, and not scared or bored.
But who killed the dogs? Who bribed my bird
With poison? Luckily there is no map
And no one ever finds me any more.

Must they all appear, awkward, to end
In the same defeat? I could not recall
Which was which any more: attitudes
Resemble, all the shadows turn to gray.
What power, what weaknesses provoke
Continuing visits and continuing pain?

I cannot answer, I can only warn.
Who comes to me with a cordial body, spine
And skull and every incidental grace,
Departs by dirty postern gate, slow,

Rumpled and no longer white or red.
You are as lovely as some, as ugly as all,

And will not linger, though absurdly brave,
Longer than the rest have stayed, but grow
Like your artful or barbaric friends
Sick and tired. Let no special sting
Offend you; it is not a personal death
At my hands you suffer, nor a private life.

On a Birthday

Wilderness precedes
    Any wisdom
Worth the name: our needs
    Are not the same

For a graveyard as
    In the forest,
But until we pass
    Among the most

Scandalous leaves, what
    Good are all these
Quaint beds, clipped and not
    Climbing? Unless

Any wasted place
    To start with is
As foul on the face
    Of it as this,

I came from the worst;
    Having entered
The tangle and got lost,
    I encountered

The local serpent
    Followed by apes,
Bears, and the red ant
    That nothing stops,

Unopposable
    In fierceness. Such
Denizens were all
    Expected, each

To be met with in
    Anybody's
Jungle. But sudden
    And unlike these

Looked-for claws and howl
    Were you, the last
I came upon, well
    Met and the first

To offer comfort:
    No less creature
For all that, a part
    Still of the bare

Trees and the twisted
    Region I live
Within—yet I would
    Swear the wood dove

Sang out, the light gained
    At our meeting,
And then all the land
    Turned from its long

Wars with the darkness
    To a clearing.
Perhaps now it is
    Still a raw thing

To claim as my own
    The orderly
Growth about me, when
    I had met the

Bright heraldic beast
        In another
Part of the forest
        Altogether,

But observing now
        The developed
Roots of days, and how
        The sun has tipped

Each conforming tree
        With autumn, is
It not wise to see
        In wilderness

The enacted course
        Of our burdens
And the greenest source
        Of all gardens?

In the Dark

To compose the reality of shadow
    Requires a light;
Even the ashes of exhausted evenings,
    Wearing the weight
And consequence of ice, glow again for some
    Kinds of coal. What
Fed the fire among such bare and broken trees
    I saw one night?
It was perhaps a dream growing in darkness
    Like the red flight
Of summer after spring: you had walked within
    The flare of bright
Torches, and the glassy particles of love
    Melted in the heat
Of every line. After you the fire died down,
    The cold was very great.

On Tour

It is the movement that disturbs the line,
  Thickening the form,
  Turning into warm
Compression what had once been cold and fine.

Seen from down here, if only we remained,
  These hills are high:
  Driving on, the sky
Imposes and no longer can be trained

By any structure of the seeming ground.
  Landscape, I discover,
  As the car gains over
Something that changes from a little mound

To monstrous eminence before your eyes,
  Landscape can flaunt, can
  Foil like a courtisan:
And when you see the difference in size

Of cliffs we once considered at the bright
  Grass along their peak
  And then saw from the bleak
Extremity of sand below, the sight

Gives more than pause—alas, it gives the slow
  Ruin of our hopes
  Fed upon the slopes
From where we've been to where we want to go.

Myopia

No matter how
Numb or practiced,
Even the most
Skillful mouths are
Merely the scars
Of love, wholly
Obedient
To the bending
Heart, hardly more
Than wounds outworn.
In the landscape
Of your crowded
Head, for instance,
Every feature
Will conform close
To a future
Weather, carving
Geologies
Of pain just where
The surprising
Lakes, monadnocks
And long ravines
Decisively
Appear, starting
Forth together
Here, to finish
Elsewhere as if
Sorted into
Separate rocks,
Clean forgotten
And far away;
There, for all we
Know of its fine

Terminations,
Our buried and
Familiar blood
Lies in a cold
Tangle—apart,
Dry, dumb. Seeing
At this distance
How flesh and bone
Must grow into
Division, chilled
Beneath the weight
Of sudden snow
And lost to their
Intended laws—
Seeing so near
The coming wreck,
I think of that
Ground we rot in
All, and stare at
The giving soil:
Faults in strata
Show like success,
Life is very
Terrible, as
Our faces know.

For S.

Music is one means of telling time
    That forces memory
To conjugate the tenses of the mind
    In terms of moving sound:
When I hear music, all I was I am.

Love, I think, has something of the same
    Effect, the other way
Around, permitting what has not yet been
    To come into its own:
With you, my love, what I will be I am.

September Twenty-Ninth

Decay is in the poplar,
    Darkness gathers
On even the simplest
    Leaf, and withers.

Never in this climate
    Of loss before
Could I have ascended
    To where you are

Standing—a place beyond
    Our foul weather
And all freezing. Yet I
    Have another

Comfort still to take, more
    Than keeping well
Or merely warm: ever
    Curious of all

Determinations, how
    Must I name this
Time and know this season?
    Like travellers

And other such strangers,
Calling places
They came to by titles
Of the countries

They had lost, can I do
Else in the wrong
Weather but look up and
Label it spring?

De Manus Fabrica

for Andreas Vesalius

Where the knuckles rise like Apennines
            From an umber undersod,
        Where the blood so abruptly loosens
All its lakes about these sudden bones,
            Apprentice, mark your lesson
With the signature of life: beneath
            A circumstantial skin, cut
        To the shrinking center of this hand.

This hand . . . It is a body without politics,
            A no man's land for the queer
        Companionable creatures that swarm
In silent flocks through every fervent cell—
            Freaks of talent, erratic
Virtuosi of the lymph, forcing
            The merest flesh to fortune
        And the mightiest to its flaw.

Only the bone is orthodox, submits
            To condemnations of the will:
        White Isolde renounces and dies
Rigid in her joy as any warp
            Of wave-whitened rib, a bone
No longer contended for by bones.
            And when Saint Catherine hung
        In splinters on her wheel, the blood

Draining off like memory, then at last
            She found the dry detachment
        Of pure desire. Now, apprentice,

Take a living hand; learn from it how
    Upon love's skeleton, within
The protocol of bones unwavering
      And white, some red imperfect
      Self must keep us wet and keep us warm.

Summer Forecast

What wind there was this morning
      And what rain
Betrayed the bitter month they met in—
      Of course there was no sun.

The darkness spared no symptom
      Of its pain,
No parturition. Whatever birth
      Might trouble the black earth

Was not to be witnessed beyond
      My own brain;
The flesh was out of question, frozen hard.
      Alone, the mind had heard

Suggestive noises: two days
      Only, but
Two marked by abandoned cold, have passed
      Clattering since I last

Was with you. For those two days
      I have not
Laid an eye, a hand, a mouth upon
      You, and stare at the wan

Prospect of as many days
      Done without
You as there will be days at all. Now,
      Ruined by rain, I know

How neglect in our season
        Of absence
Changes to weight of terrible frost,
        And I guess how the first

Or even the ultimate
        Evidence
Of loss grows light in charitable
        Weather: then will the free

Enterprise of a green earth
        Draw my sense
Down to a common fall, overthrown
        While the sun looks on, cooks on.

The Passions Discover and Declare They Do Not Create Their Occasion

Of the four elements
        only fire destroys,
Proving what we warm to
        in the winter as
A reassuring sign
        of life and increase
Is merely the bright rack
        and ruin of our
Broken world. I would take
        another emblem—
Say salt, to awaken
        the various grace
And flavor of the field
        I walk in now. But
No sowing, even to blind
        depths in the furrow,
Can bring one sprout from salt.
        Though my rough weeds grow
Into savor by its
        mediation, which
Can flourish long in such
        blank epitome?
Where is a source, a well?
        What rain I cry for
Cools the rancid weather?
        Even though you give
Water to drown my salt,
        dissolve such embers,
Still am I white in my
        mineral burning,

Or in cinder blackened:
    these ashes prevail.
Turn my tables today
    and the root I eat
Is bitter; burn down my
    house tomorrow, what
Will I carry away?
    I would save the fire.

Lyrics from Gaiety, a Farce

Waking wild-eyed in the morning
    I remember how we met,
How the records needed turning
    And the oven wouldn't shut.
Everyone enjoyed the party
    Though: they stayed till after three
(It was hellish in the city
    And my drinks were strong. And free).

When the neighbors phoned at midnight
    To complain about the noise,
I replied (so grandly!) "Drop it
    In the mailbox with the keys."
Half the cigarettes were drowned when
    Helen spilled the best champagne:
Damned if Larry's ever going to
    Make me ask that girl again!

All the tables need restaining
    Where the parakeet was "sick";
Someone left the water running
    And the kitchen is a wreck!
Two umbrellas in the closet
    Never were (or will be) mine.
I must make a little visit
    To my bank right after ten.

Meanwhile, reckoning a shambles
    That is worthy of Pompeii,
Where the melted ice resembles
    All that's left of Lidice,

I recall the ancient order
    Which presided when you came—
How you happily regarded
    The appointments of my home.

Now you're lying in the bedroom
    And your face is rather gray,
Its expression—what an emblem
    Of the dreams of yesterday!
I apologize for dinner
    (Only two or three were ill)
—You will find the bromoquinine
    In the bathroom down the hall.

The Penates have disowned us,
    And some other gods as well
Have explicitly abandoned
    What remains of mortal will.
Undisguised by easy living
    In the difficult light of dawn,
"Man's Estate" in there is having
    Trouble staying in his skin.

If the Powers that plumped our pillow
    And contrived this bedding-down
Gave a thought to what must follow,
    How amused they might have been:
Once the sacred passions climax
    And the proud *afflatus* goes,
How unwieldy these poor relics—
    Purely human mysteries.

Floating, face up, on the open
     Estuary
Of sleep, you wait for it to happen.
     You are very

Beautiful, stupid, and alone
     Now at the source
Of all the loneliness we learn
     From someone else.

For you the darkness does its part—
     Arms fall, and eyes,
And the heart proves by its lack an art
     The mouth supplies.

Sleep then, or feign to, as you drown
     And I pursue
Your blood to its filthy cellar down
     In the hollow

Hairy places. Here shall I feed
     Where every sense,
Handmaid and Hangman to your need,
     Is audience.

III   MUSICIAN'S SONG

Some we know play trumpets
     In a public place;
Some to please extend their knees
     Around a double bass.

Some discover concord
    In a perfect fourth;
Some from cellos, some from bellows
    Make their money's worth.
Some I've heard played loudly
    (They were not the best);
One or two—none sweet as you—
    Played sweeter than the rest.

Cautious critics tell us
    In the pieces prized
Virtuosos never rose so
    High as advertised;
Better choose a program
    Something less than pro—
Connoisseurs, like amateurs,
    Listen while they blow.

IV   DUET FOR THREE VOICES

Primo: O whom are you fooling
        Said Failure to Phony
    What role do you covet
        You never could play?

Secundo: I ride on a carrousel
        Carrying many:
    I want what the others
        Have given away.

Primo: And how are you feeling
        Said Feral to Failure
    What acts have you witnessed
        What work have you done?

Secundo: Sometimes I regret as I
                    Sulk in my cellar
            How much, as I watch them,
                    I hate every one.

Primo: Whose cup are you filling
                    Said Phony to Feral
            What kind of a doorknob
                    Can turn you, my man?

Secundo: In bed where my practice
                    Is openly plural
            I seldom leave early—
                    Do come if you can.

Una Voce: The night that is falling
                    Confirms our disguises
            Determines our calling
                    And darkens our grief.

            For Failure what future
                    For Phony what prizes
            For Feral what creature
                    Can sanction our life?

                    V   BAWD'S SONG

            Our talk in bars is inexact
                    Slurring the heart's
                    Verb in respect

To voice or person, and exhorts
A tropic motion
In the parts

Needing most refrigeration.
Orderly kinds
Of passion

Come elsewhere—upon our minds
Of course, come
Like old wounds

Covering up their bloody time.
But now and here
Is a scheme

And a scandalous semaphor
Improvable
By no mere

Elocutionary skill:
What diction so
Final and full

As a mouth unfastening into
One such perfect
Empty O?

VI   BLUES

Leaving late I lock up lit
Stammering slightly
Quite unsightly

49

And half seas over—profligate:
                I'm so far out
                Of limits that I lately
Relinquish my footing completely,
                And this almost nightly.

Time that once consoled us both
                For all our bother
                Now, I gather,
Devises gin and dry vermouth
                (In Wine is Truth)
                To jostle us together,
Just one damned thing after another
                In a changing weather.

Often reft when left behind
                The mind will wander
                Wide and slander
Even its own. If mine is found
                Floating around
In your flat beer or under
The bar, after taking a gander,
                Please Return to Sender.

                VII   ISLAND BLUES

        Lost my love
        on one of
                the Thousand Islands
        (wherever
        a river
                goes there are islands).
        If you are

                        50

together
    each of the islands
makes a kind
of mainland.
    Otherwise islands
divide and
conquer. Find
    my love: no islands
for me. Lost
my love last
    night on the islands—
    the Thousand Islands.

The Gardener to his Thumb, Once Green

It is a bare and crooked
    Tree to heaven
      Growing,
Lovelier perhaps for showing
    Black; but naked
      Even
    So to hold
Such narrow helping from the cold.

I walk round it when I can
    (Barely so smooth,
      So straight
Myself), comforted to equate
    The life of man
      Thus with
    Another's—
Even one that rots or withers.

The branches tremble; living,
    It is never
      The less
A tree such as I could possess,
    A law giving
      Over:
    Not to be,
But becoming; less safe—more free.

In the white season I found
    Proud ornaments
      Pasted
On it. But look how these rusted

Metal pears grind
        Poor dents
        In the bark,
Bending the raw twigs fork from fork!

Someone passes—who is it
        Comes now, noble
                Creature:
Is it the King of Spain's daughter
        Come to visit
                Me, all
        For the sake
Of my one black tree? Take it back

To Spain! Flourish among almonds,
        My ill-hung tree;
                Impart
To her a less ironic fruit
        Than what you once
                Bore me.
        I shall wreathe
Another tree now (barely smooth

Or straight myself) with gold pears
        That cannot waste;
                They grow
Only mortal ones in Spain. How
        Many these tears,
                And lost
        All to win
A tree? Better leave off. No. Begin!

Landed: A Valentine

See how the brown kelp withers in air
    Gasping to its death
Upon the salty ice. A moment
    Only was enough
To banish the loveliness that made
    Of a few rather
Inexpressive weeds under water
    A lover's emblem
Of success—easy-moving, soft and
    In the heart's color.

Can simple air become so foul? Now
    After a short time
Parted from warm company we kept
    Together, I share
That condition, a gradual rot
    So far from the sea:
Absence of the proper element
    Will take effect, take
Soon the mouth out of my very words.

Motto on a garden clock
Referring to the twelve hours:
OMNES VULNERANT, NECAT

ULTIMA. Stand close to me
While the sun lasts. By losses
Sustained we come to this grief,

Learning here in a shadow
How we figured—how we shall
Erase. But the last one kills,

The remembered: ULTIMA
NECAT, the sun is going
Down, the faces dim, the dark . . .

A Place out of the Sun

Weakness you called it
To cherish this cairn
Of exhausted rocks
I live on, plucking
Quartz from quartz for earth.
Already you left
Your own such mountain,
Had passed along down
The steep eminence
Of old affections,
To discover, sole,
A private landscape
In the plains below.
That is one country
I have never seen,
But can imagine
How you struck terror
And delight upon
The inhabitants,
Casting your shadow
Like a persistent
Obelisk laid low
And long as the sun
Would lengthen it. If
The sun moved, why then
The shadow moved too,
And you never had
Twice the same bed to
Lie in, rest being
Ruin, boredom, fear.
But something stopped you

Once, here you are: can
Weakness hold you now?
I wonder. Though I
Have seldom foraged
From these stones, I grow
Fresh in abiding shade,
And from blue places
Underneath, who knows
What surprising growth
To greet, provided
Shadows stay on me—
Whether broken or whole
I care not, but stay.

Agreement with Sir Charles Sedley

Accommodating love with "something still
    Of the sea," he only meant
    To decorate a failure spent
Upon Corinna's bed, from which he went
Away too suddenly to serve it well.

Yet with her for an hour the Cavalier
    Discovered comfort from the cold,
    And found it politic to hold
A warming world against him, though he told
Corinna's maid to call him well before

The King would ride, and time itself return.
    The lovers closeted apace
    And fell together—an embrace
That gathered each unbidden sense to grace,
Though not the kind Corinna's fan could learn.

Thereat the summons of a little bell
    Inconsiderately spread
    Silver tumult overhead.
Corinna laughed, and tidied up her bed;
The laureate subsided with the swell.

In truth love had a semblance of the sea,
    Showing less among the fair
    Ripples of Corinna's hair
Than sharing in the ignorant and bare
Condition of its wreck: a breaking free.

Corinna stirred. She was alone, so closed
    Her cabinet. Perhaps she thought
    How Venus' beauty had been wrought
To birth upon the ocean, later caught
With Mars in Vulcan's net. Corinna dozed.

That night, at Margate, the low water ran
    White on every knocking stone,
    Embittered almost, as if one
God more were gone. It was the very tone
And timbre—somewhat louder—of a man.

The Shepherd Corydon

Having for some time heard
Nightly in low places
Of incomparable
Creatures that had been hung
Imaginatively
On my heart, disguising
There the boring body
Of a poor impostor,
Having attended to
Whatever bad rumors
Ran among your hopes as
In your most hopeless fears,
You must have expected
The hooded Basilisk
Itself, or the Hydra
Whose rubbery heads are
Likely to penetrate
Anywhere, and supposed
At least the Chimaera
(Which is known for its frauds)
To be among the stale
Myths of a monstrous me.

And this was a mistake.
Later, when you were so
Warmly obliged to give
Away your old fancies,
Was it not difficult
To face the hard choices,
Hating as you did to
Abandon the legend,
The crumbled fairy tales,

In favor of one fact—
The raw rough animal?

Where and to what purpose
Was the story then? Where,
Finding yourself at last
Here, down, and darkened by
A furious human
Creature in a foreign
Skin—where was the bright news,
The chronicle of day?

On the sighing bed, boy,
Something changes the past.
Fictions, even yours, turn
Over and expose. You
Became the myth I was
The moment that I came;
More collapsed with the warm
Deceit than is to be
Recovered: Glaucon or
Antinous—someone
Other!
        And terrible
That I, no magic left
Now, by daylight, discover
You, dead, anonymous
After the night, and cold
In your flesh against me . . .

Continuing

Manners of this time this place
    moderate me.
Weather grows accustomed, space
    more or less free
To take whatever shape you left
    in the soft air,
Memories of the eyeball fixed
    but not forced there.

It is an anyhow world
    I wander, run
Now to such days, corroding, cold
    for the season
But never too white for spring.

The Return from Montauk

"Staring at the east
Behind the windows of our train,
What is it you see at nightfall?"

"I can see something . . .
It is the falling sun, wrongly
Reflected on this pale heaven,

A red suicide
Descending where, before, the hopes
Of every day mounted to their

Customary wreck.
Looking out with you through the clear
Deception of a moving train,

I see the sunset
Spread upon the east that should be
Blue as any water, just as

With another eye
I see, in the brilliant glass,
Love, like another sun, rising
      In the western sky."

Prospects of Another Summer
in the Hamptons

I found the same shell, with a frayed root
Grown to strange distortion gripping it,
That I had kicked farther down the beach
Last August. Now, a winter afterward,
Could I, a proper student of the sand,
  Distinguish what was quick
   From corruption?

The valves had not yet quite relinquished
Their hold, adhered still, though only air
Filled their wrecked ovals, and the vise
Of whitened roots that clasped them close
Had suffered from the salt as surely
  As this shell was empty:
   Death hugging death

For dear life, while maybe four feet off
The waves indulged that same display
Of orderly dishevelment I could not fit
My senses to, the skin of dirty lace
Dissolving in a deeper glow of green.
  It was the root-bound shell,
   Mortality,

I remembered while the living water ran
Out of mind, and I forgot the sea.
What will summer be besides a grave
Unless everything we forget, even life,
Makes what we are, just as much
  As anything, even death,
   We remember?

For a Book of Hours

I   AN APRIL AT THE CHÂTEAU DOURDAN

The lady's hand holding a buttercup
Confesses by its bloom against its bud
The beauty of relations still unripe.

Listen, gentles, before the clouds parade
Their music, here's a sharper music come;
A will worth something more than all your game
Of indigo gowns and feathers in the sun
Freshens the espaliers and commends
To ivy the old walls they grow upon—
Something more than a lilac lover
Bends her hand, her garment, and that bright trefoil:

It is the Garden, lady. This is where
Beneath the arches and the spangled air
You fell before the simple earth was full.

II   POL DE LIMBOURG RIDES TO AVIGNON IN MAY

Even the grass bore blossoms and the sun
Rang like a sound of music in the mind,
That day we crossed the woods to Avignon.
Upon the journey, gay and green, we chose
Appropriate amours, and when the wind
Flattered the pale ascent of sycamores
In like ascensions sighing, we discerned
Our journey's lesson in its broken phrase.

Here is a world of bright venereals,
Eager in dominion, opulent
But muted too, whose compromising wills

Accord the count his countess and shall prove
Their match beyond all fops of temperament:

Love is the color of a lady's sleeve.

III   TO JEAN BOURDICHON AT THE OCTOBER SOWING

Beyond those intricate mountains, well beyond
The river in the barley fields where men
And orderly oxen are, the Scorpion

Reaches for a charred and bitter ground
To poison, some unyielding interval
When swans no longer double in the pond
And Anjou is a not quite physical land;

As if the claw of some white principle
Had torn away the unnecessary gold
And with it all our grandiose moving green.

Say then that the zodiac runs on
And that there are not leaves enough to hold—
No matter, Jean, that the ambitious fields grow cold:
The fat is in the fire, the summer sown!

Address Unknown

Hurrying the tired heart
From worry tonight homeward
And fast over hills beyond
Here to somewhere eagerly
Else, love, run, run to your rest.

Standing stock-still I marvel
How much you so resemble
The imp of promises I
At best improvidently
Took you for in old weather . . .

Comes the broken time, labels
Even of a light travel
Lie as of a dark. Look how
The burning countries oh far
Away grow black down again

67

Cock-a-Doodle-Do!

Change in our weather
Wakened me, the winter struck a chord
Upon its crooked instrument, an owl
Diminished: nothing dared to move.
My clock suggested but it did not tell,
And if there was no witness who could prove
There was a crime? Look how an angry bird
Blackened my bed this morning with the smell
Of burning feathers!

Not the famous fowl
But a lesser phoenix that has left
These ashes in my sheets; I burn him up
To find the creature fire and fear again—
Fire in his hair, fear in his absent cup,
Rara avis! I wonder if the pain
Of April warming on his wings will sift
Such dirty cinders; or will they all drop
Down to make fools

Of the sleepy five
That were my senseless senses. Senses fail;
Observe the hinting clock, the hollow sound
Of music in the dark, then sympathize
With all the birds that celebrate the end
For which they first were made: whatever size
Our incandescent rooster, he must fill
The cavity of sorrow to commend
The whole of love.

68

Sandusky—New York

*If you have received well
you are what you have received.*

Ohio from a train
Looked always other; half his way across
    The unimportant chain
Of Alleghenies that intended east.
    An early morning rain
Made dubious the sky and in its stead,
    As if all hope were gone
Of reckoning climate by his calendar,
    Ran April like a stain
Across the glass—unfinished, unfulfilled
    And frankly alien.

As in the past, today
Landscape and weather were his enemies;
    It seemed unlikely they
Would yield. But if in answer to their terms
    Of terror he could say
For sure how mountains fell from monstrous size
    To minor lumps of clay
Behind his eyes, how every season turned
    Within his heart to gray:
This once, perhaps, the darkness too would fall
    In less pronounced a way.

He thought how many times
He had construed the weather like a verb,
    Declined the rain, that comes
As water will—unasked, but a forgiven guest—
    And even in his dreams
Had pressed a grammar on the land. Somehow

They were important themes,
Such wet beginnings as he knew, this earth
That April never seems
To satisfy, the sullen passage of
His unprotesting homes.

Distance made the weather
Disappear. The clouds that filled the sky
Conformed until they were
Illustrious with being. Time was before
Him, no need to hurry
Understanding. Where the towns had loomed
Dark with incoherence
Of houses, the primary colors, after rain,
Startled him to praise. Here
The land grew lovely in the stillness of
Accumulated air,

As one would have it first,
Not later hope occasionally; here
The sun, that had abused
His eyes a moment by the distances
Of moving mountains, placed
Perspectively the shoulders of the earth,
Discovered as he passed
The consequentialities of weed
And water moving west
Against his progress, while his purpose grew
Within him like an East.

Such travelling was true
In parallel. Along the simple tracks
Which accurately flew

Beneath, he followed himself away, away
    From weather came into
That unconditional country of his blood
    Where even landscape grew
Dim as he had never dared to hope,
    And when he breathed he knew
The air as sick men breathe and know the spring:
    Cold still, but coming to.

    Now, the train running on,
He clambered up the enterprising bones
    His body reached him down
So carefully for the ascent, he climbed
    The scaffold skeleton
Up shoulders to the summit of his skull
    (Past marshes overgrown
And hollows filled by sudden rubbishes)
    Until he stared upon
The shore of all his history, as it
    Would look when it was done.

    The clumsy body, where
He had before been always caught, imposed
    An image of its care
Upon the country's custom, made him feel
    (Generous in passing for
Pausing in passing): *only when you leave*
    Will you know where you are.
He travelled, putting distance into sense.
    The mountains fell, and far
Ahead he thought he saw the sea. What if
    It was, if it was there?

Then that was where, tonight
He wanted to arrive. Thus he would leave
The suburbs of his heart,
Would come to the capital city where it was.
The sun became as bright
Above him as the sight could bear. He knew
It then, that he would find
The fabulous city and the fact of seas
Already in his mind,
And only there: the landscape lived in him
As he might live in it.

DAMAGES

To Sanford Friedman
The mind certain of its meat
The heart's law undisputed

I

A Far Cry After a Close Call

For if they do these things in a green tree what
shall be done in the dry?
                        —*Luke* 23:31.

Nuns, his nieces, bring the priest in the next
Bed pralines, not prayers for the next world,
        But I've had one look myself
            At *that* one (looking

Back now, crammed in the convalescent ward,
With the invisible man opposite
        Sloshing most of the Black Sea
            Around in his lungs,

While the third patient coughs and borrows *Time*).
No one turned over when I was wheeled in;
        The efficient British nurse
            Snipped off my soggy

Trousers and put me right, "sure as Bob's your
Uncle." The water roared and ran away,
        Leaving only words to stock
            My mind like capsules

Crowding a bottle. Then the lights blew up,
Went out, someone was going through My Things
        While I rowed—rowed for my life
            Down the rubber floor—

75

But the waves failed me. The hallway heaved where I
Foundered and turned in my doctor's dry hands
      To sovereign selflessness:
         Meaning had melted.

"*Mon corps est moi,*" Molière said. They're more than that,
This monster the body, this miracle
      Its pain — when was I ever
         Them, when were they me?

At thirty-three, what else is there to do
But wait for yet another great white moth
      With eager, enlarging eyes
         To land on my chest,

Slowly, innocently choking me off?
The feelers stir while I lie still, lie here
      (Where on earth does it come from,
         That wind, that wounding

Breath?), remembering the future now,
Foreseeing a past I shall never know,
      Until the little crisis
         Breaks, and I wake.

For as Saint Paul sought deliverance from
The body of this death, I seek to stay —
      Man is mad as the body
         Is sick, by nature.

Seferiades: A Poem in Two Parts

For Michael Lekakis

i

How much like life itself, to know
    his midwest translator, not
the Middle-Eastern troglodyte
    shambling onto the platform
led by my suave scholarly friend.
    Later, when his own turn came,
I was to learn if not the source
    of what had doused me, at least
then the delta it headed for,
    a plausible jet of all
that heroic jabber. Now we were
    just marking time until it
ran by us, not even words but
    a welter of speech dissolved
in a watery idiom.
    Afterwards would come the words,
the tragic cosmopolitan
    lies, lessons from an exile,
Smyrna oranges and laments.
    The famous foreign poet
mounted the stream of utterance:
    his palms, an oily capital,
propped that marble head, enormous,
    stained brown like ruins, rocking
mournfully on his round shoulders,
    measuring the monologue
of an old man's voice that dribbled
    out of an old woman's mouth.

Twitching in the chair beside me,
      the Greek I had invited
for comfort, a cushion against
      my Barbarian's conscience,
whispered to himself, while Something
      spoken on the stage extracted
from his hands, that lay like mallets
      in his lap, the convulsive
gestures of protest or pleasure—
      I could not tell, but only
that habits had been changed, hidden
      or laid bare, and still the Voice
which was a waste to me, to him
      ecstasy caught in its act,
ran on, the Poem persisting
      whenever its syllables
threatened to dissolve in the sands
      of a cadence completed.
Abruptly, in that guttural
      wilderness (not one meaning
but a movement among meanings
      possible), I recognized—
desperate, no doubt, for a hold
      on any knowledge—the word
for "river," then the word for "sun."
      And as in life, when the words
come, the meanings waken: "River . . .
      Sun." I waited for the rest.

Obscure behind the lectern where
      the laureate subsided
but would not be still, inveighing
      against silence as against
"Izmir," the willing translator

78

waited, licked his lips, ready
though the alien voice prevailed,
    the bald dome careening, eyes
down and darkened, into discourse.
    Peering at my friend, whose part
was yet to come, where he hovered
    like a cape of qualms behind
that Mediterranean headland,
    I waited too, suddenly
discovering I knew the word
    for "man" and the word for "life"
and the word for "river" again.
    Then, many times, the word for
"god" came, and just as suddenly
    it was over, the old Greek
clawing at the mike they had draped
    around his neck on a dead
garland, and even our applause
    could not drown out his choking;
my friend the bearded professor
    offered to help, but the Master
fought him off, won free, and waved him
    to the stand he stumbled from.

Now it was not so much like life,
    but I could make out the words,
all of them, in a long lament
    about Helen, false Helen
who was not at Troy—a linen
    undulation there, a thing
of air—while Mrs. Menelaus
    languished, for real, on the Nile
—not Ilion but her nails ruined
    by a brown river, the sun

baking an empty land, "on the lip
    of Egypt," and Paris lay
with nothing more than a shadow,
    and the others were slaughtered
for nothing, for a Helen's sake.
    Then came the place where the word
for "god" had been lisped so often:
    "O nightingale, nightingale,"
my friend read out cold, careful not
    to try for a rhapsode's tone,
the typed sheet trembling a little
    in his hands: "O nightingale!
(three times, *aïdóni*, to the ear
    anonymous) What is a god?
What is not a god? What is the life
    in between god and not-god?"
Unwreathed beside him, the old man
    nodded: that was how it went;

that was the claim he recognized,
    a clamor in the mind, so
he knew what came next, the end came:
    "And messengers were sent off
to tell him, when their lungs allowed,
    how much suffering, so much
of life had fallen from the light,
    so much into the abyss,
and all for a shifting garment,
    for no more than a Helen."
Again the applause, but this time
    as if our hands understood
what to our ears before had been
    the wrong tide of sound turning.
The diffident reader deferred,

abashed, to clapping that washed
over the old head like a stream
    caressing a brown boulder
in its boisterous course. Beside me
    the Greek was up, murmuring
something about a myth, and rushed
    back to embrace the poet,
both of them crying, and in all
    that crowd of gratulating
Hellenes bearing gifts, what better
    could I do than ask my Greek
to come and meet my friend, his friend's
    American translator?

ii

Across the little lake, a mile
    from where we were standing, stark
against the fingernail of sand
    that scarred our summer's blue frieze,
we could still see her, a moving
    figure, tiny now and black
at this distance as she was blond
    close up, close to the color
of her tremulous beach, the mild
    sublime that in the Maine air
beckoned still, opposite our dock.
    Six of us, tired blue-lipped boys,
traded rabbit punches between
    goose pimples, staring hard
over the water all that while
    we were waiting for our coach
to tell us the time we had made,
    impatient though for more

than our trophies, peering
  across the twice-lapped lake, less
a medium now than a mood,
  at the mysterious dame
who had met us there and offered
  jasmine tea, toadstools that came
apart before we could take them
  from her long white hands—but then
suddenly she had sent us home
  like boys. Or did we escape?

In any case, we got away,
  happy now we had taken
the chance, the test, the rehearsal
  of ourselves thrusting us on:
swimming the mile over, the mile
  back, one odd hour's rest between—
one hour at best outside the shack
  of the weirdo in the woods.
She fed us, humming to herself,
  touching Jimmy where his suit
sagged, playing with him just like that:
  "What is all this juice and all
this joy?" And who knew what to say?
  Now, after the lake, the planks
burned, and where their shadows landed
  on its pea-green surface, boulders
showed between the slats: we could see
  fish in their slow enterprise,
as if the water really was
  a weaker form of ice. The sun
drew circles on the lake, their rim
  being that scalp of white sand
before which her shawls hung upon

the wind, imitating still
the gestures of our crawl, the way
      a man puts on the shadow
he walks into. She had spoken . . .
      to all of us? to Jimmy? me?

"The cup," she said, "drink this, it will
      make you immortal—take it."
Remembering, we laughed at her,
      a mile away and only
a nature-creep now, some kind of
      fae in the forest. Eager
for our counsellor to inspect,
      we shouldered each other to
the brink, searching for places where
      immortality would show
first. Little waves smacked at the dock:
      underneath the boards the wood
was slimy, rotting, cold. Jimmy
      shivered, and just then our coach
appeared, working down the hillside
      to the dock, whistle bobbing
on the lanyard around his neck,
      the sun by now powerless
against his brown bald head. Never
      hurrying, he just happened
to be wherever it was hoped,
      and when: a man left over
from an age when the old men lived
      and the young men died. I told
him what had happened, or I told
      what the six of us thought
had happened: they were not the same
      stories, but he heard them out.

"Each of you drank," he said. "Now which . . ."
　　　and set to work, confident
we would not betray our chances
　　　of divinity, for all
the ridicule we had mustered.
　　　Wisest of men, he devised
a graver stratagem: at once
　　　his hands, withered by water
more than by the years, sounded out
　　　our bodies, easy over
the clammy limbs, expert, depraved,
　　　relentless, palpating where
the portal skin lay slack, prying
　　　at the reluctant muscles,
smoothing flesh where it would pucker
　　　and the hair, already rough
in hollows where it soon would curl.
　　　"She said it would make us gods
if we didn't tell!" Donald shrieked,
　　　and the old man nodded, hands
languid, sure. He had been across
　　　the lake, our sullen weedy
watering place; had visited
　　　as others were probably
visiting now—why else had she
　　　dismissed us?—a witches' world,
the site we have all, at one time,
　　　discovered, created, lost.

For this he was our waterfront
　　　familiar, rummaging now
among our bones sleeved in their still
　　　uncertain flesh distempered
by scratches, bites, sliding over

scars already blurred by tan,
an old man talking to himself,
    as one grudging the future
to what is of no use to him,
    until he straightened and spoke
to the six, naked before him,
    cuffing the last boy in line:
"Silly as you are, stunned by what
    she has done or made you do,
bruised by a lurching behavior
    like the lake's, sore from the loss
of what you left behind, you pocked
    peeling children, even so"—
and the solemn words met and moved
    in our minds like speaking lips—
"not one boy among you could I
    dare to single out and say,
'You, my friend, you are not a god.'"
    Across the water, the beach
winced now and wrinkled in the glare:
    she was going away and
we could see her going; once gone,
    the sun's white circle widened.

Secular Games

Levin, on his way to Kitty's love,
Saw children walking in a row to school,
Bluish doves flying down from the eaves
And little floury loaves thrust out
By an unseen hand. "It all happened at once,"
Tolstoy says: a boy ran suddenly
Toward a dove and glanced back, smiling,
At Levin. The dove flew up, wheeling,
And the snowflakes glittered in the sun.
From the windows came a smell of fresh bread
And the loaves were put out. Remember?
So much grace Tolstoy grants without God.

"It all happened at once," once at midnight
In that unseasonable fall of ours —
It seemed to me the universe slowed down
And lingered in a climate of its choice
As if without the Law. I had a sense
Of something ceded, something given over
In that bad autumn, when day after day
The city warmed, its summer smells restored
To a tempting lie. All our sparrows stayed
While even migratory birds confined
Their circulation, did not go, but hung
Upon the hindered weather like a curse.

I reached our crooked corner where the night
Unwinds. Like Levin, I was on my way.
Slowly the citizens moved past, so many
Allegories of choice, most of them gay
As bright October's wreck or brazenly
Concealing the winter to come. Over us loomed
The ladies' prison where The Girls called down
Inaccurate obscenities to us

Or to each other, inside out. Above
Our 'rescued' Ruskin courthouse roof
The tower held its numb Gothic dial
Gold as a medal against the dim sky.

There I stood among The Boys, marvelling
While they murmured by me like a stream
Beneath the shouting girls, shorn Rapunzels
In their castle keep, and stared above
At the clock, at the unfeeling sky
Above even that, wondering what wind
Bearded with snowflakes like Tolstoy's God
Could carry off our grief, could save us
Or by leaving soothe? Was liberty
To leave enough? It was enough to stay,
To inhabit earth, where we do not stay
But unlike God in heaven, come and go.

"So, if I Dreame
I Have You, I Have You"

First I had a dream of water,
  then one of rotting.
Your eyes, loosened from their arches,
  were salt ponds, sinking,
and your lips opened like a sluice:
  I failed to follow
the juice where it ran down, rinsing
  a deeper hollow.

The decaying dream worked upward—
  this time I could not
bear to see a jelly taking
  your face, fast, away.
But waking, I extol waking,
  for I cannot call
you to mind without energy:
  movements of making.

I have the will to win over
  rot and water both,
to recover dreams by turning
  them true, thus earning
back what I spent by night. Coming
  is a coming to,
learning by the body's wet spoil
  to endure morning.

Seeing Cousin Phyllis Off

The SS France, *Second Class, Cabin* U–20

Few sights were lovelier
Than my watch laved in the *brut* champagne
Exploding from a jiggled magnum.
Your foreign cabin-mates' *schadenfreude*
        Helped them help each other
        To more caviar, and your handsome
        Husband brushed me off, as handsome does;
Wizened by a decade of adultery,
        You whispered some final
        Instructions under the din, patted
        Your graying bun: for a dozen years
The sacred fount had been flowing in his
        Favor, and you knew it.
        In Paris, a daughter was pregnant,
        Unmarried, impatient for your next
Round of meddling to begin. The cycle
        Of all our messy lives
        Alters so little from war to war
        I wonder how any of us
Dares to hope for a private happiness.
        Wilde said what we want is
        Pleasure, not happiness—it has more
        Tragic possibilities. Your caviar
Must be second-class too: I miss the old
        Normandie, Narrenschiff
        Of our fashionable thirties. Now
        The diesels suddenly start to throb
In a sickening vibrato that drives
        The implacable screw
        Up through even the *pont supérieur.*

89

My stomach turns, but all the champagne
Is gone, except for the foam in my watch,
　　　I nod at the nightmare
　　　Of a class that we both belong to:
　　　Repetition, and hurry away
To give your worried lover messages.
　　　　My poor mad Cousin Phyl,
　　　No use trying to drown time on these
　　　Harridan voyages of ours—once
They called them maiden—not by wet watches
　　　Or even dry champagne.

To Aegidius Cantor

Inculpated for heresy before the Episcopal Court at Cambrai, 1411

Only you would find it easy to believe
    What we are about these days
Or at least these nights, for little that we do
    Is likely to amaze you,
Minister who flung open the doors of your
    Adamite conventicle
And having suffered the high inspiration
    Of the Holy Ghost (the which
Visited you as you lay with the Brethren
    In quivering chastity),
Ran out into the street, "a long way stark
    Naked," wearing on your head
A platter of meat. It must have been a dark
    Village whose urbanity
You ruffled, while our town of course is klieg-lit
    Wherever there might be cause
For danger. Yet if we didn't go you one
    Better, then we went as far
Lately, arranging to have our chargers full
    Of fish, flesh and fowl, bloody
Sausages and all, dump in a lumpy stream
    Upon the bodies of six
Bikini-bare girls and boys disporting there
    On stage—the lineaments
Of galvanized desire—painting each other
    Pleonastically red,
And we labelled it "Meat Joy." A Happening.

It is because events, for us, are sacred
        In themselves, without the need
For any concentrated sign, any Writ,
        That I wanted to write you
(To whom our dim question: "Yes, but is it art?"
        Would never have occurred);
To us, you see, it is what occurs that counts,
        That becomes art — *we* call *art*
Holy these days, which is why we are concerned
        With what it is. No longer
Just theater, though the catharsis was there,
        More than fun, it was a physick
You set out to serve, patching the sick pavements
        Of Cambrai with blood. The power
Of your nakedness, metaphor of the meat
        You wore as a kind of crown,
The charismatic carnal emanations
        Not only from the salver
But from yourself — white skin, black hair, the limbs
        We see in Bosch and Cranach —
Such things could heal. And it is healing we seek,
        An art that will medicine
To selfhood and malnutrition of impulse.
        We covet your conception,
After our comical ways, for there is one
        Knowledge shared: we know the health
Of the City cannot be secret. Raw meat
        Serves, when served up in the raw,
To remind us of the life running under
        The hairy skin, red that must
Keep us comfortable by being kept inside.
        Few deign to show, or dare to,
Where it keeps, and yet the blood is there, helping
        Matters happen all the time;

Small wonder we revere the occurrences
  That spatter our streets with gore—
Mere events, call them, performances, ventures
  Which having been made become
The going on of things, the enduring flow.

  Take another time, to wit
One April in Paris, Dali dropped an ox
  Flayed and dripping to the stage
As emblematic climax to a ballet
  Among the gasps and greasy
Legs of girls, the painted drops still running while
  The curtain fell, and the riot
Which followed surprised no one, of course. Silly,
  That sympathetic magic
Must have seemed to you, but inevitable
  To carnivores, and meaning,
For all our burlesque, much what you had in mind:
  Human love resists the body
It inhabits, its old enemy and friend.
  Cantor, I remember you
And prize your heretic episode the more
  Because I praise what we do:
There is a pitch past cruelty as past love
  When all flesh acquires the same
Queer smell. Then the order of our blood commands,
  Enforces a discipline
Though never a predictable one. Say
  It is the mess we live by,
Made into a joy. The meat joy. You know. Thanks.

The Lover Showeth Wherefore He Is Abandoned of the Beloved He Sometime Enjoyed, Even in Sleep

Tonight (the moonless kind
That Judith might have spent
In Holofernes' tent
Until her ravished victim found
His final ravishment)
The many come to mind
Who lately came and, coming, later went,

Taking a way you must
Soon take yourself, I trust,
While by the brazen laws
That league diversion with disgust
Those others plead their cause
Elsewhere, to the applause
I lavished best when they deserved it least.

I lean now on your bed
And trace a pulsing vein
That proves you are not dead:
Dividing us, that other Red
Sea dandles you within
Its tides until you deign
To wake and make the sea divide again.

Each of us peers into
Mirrors for what is true
About the rest: mostly
We spend our spare time in the blue
Movies of memory.
We are blind seeing, see
Blind, and find our way the way moles do.

Moved but unmoving, I
  Sit here and stare your sleep
  Out of countenance. My
Crude hopes crumble to a heap
  As retrospectively
  I sift what I would keep
Of all such savored, severed fellowship:

  Tall in my mind stands one
  (I seldom heard him speak)
  Whose only lifelong work
Was burnishing the boyhood on
  His face; and one whose look
  I know, though I have known
No likes of him: unlikely guest, he's gone

  (Our neighborly disgrace)
  Without a proper name;
  Here's one I had for whom
No second act, or try, or time
  Was real; another whose
  Fortunes went up in flame—
His ghost, among the ghosts, in ashes goes.

  But let the darkness fall
  Politely on them all:
  The past must have an end.
Your dreaming body and my mind
  Alone at last contend.
  Courageously I send
My thought against you while your mute limbs loll

  At enviable ease.
  You lie without surprise

Beside me as I wait
For clues: the file is incomplete.
    Who is it that you meet
    When your round shoulders rise
And shed your hands like dead leaves on the sheet?

    You sigh and smile and seem
    Released. I ask you where
    You've been. What is the home
You visit while in exile here?
    As if you couldn't care
    Less (your record is clear)
You answer in a trance, "I never dream."

Eusebius to Florestan: On Aprosexia

Prince, pity me then, for it is an ill
Uncircumstanc'd save as the air inscribes,
When if I lose the tenth of what I have
I'm lost. After comes a time when if I keep
The tenth of what I have I shall be saved;
Even as the lamb that feeds on what
Has melted in the mouth, runs down
Into the heart, and cannot name the taste.

Prince, what days are these! I stare
Into the sun with hatred, it will make
The winter worse. Mortality
And the dim senses are my reason only.
There is no dark endeavor in my love,
But lately when I look'd into your eyes
That gleam like incandescent grapes
Or listen'd to the sounds, ling'ring still,
Of your speech within my ear, echoings
I have not had since Word was made Flesh,
It was as if I sudden saw the waves
Obey when I struck the sea and said: Take me!

Happiness is an embarrassment (men say,
In truth, that the material world is but
A fiction, though any other is nightmare).
Thereto so unsuited am I that my bearing,
Prince, grows awkward if it is too great:

The peacock would be overcome by glory
Were he not accustom'd to it from the start.
Today I have search'd my solitude, Prince,
For your grace, but a man's genius is wearied
By the habit of hoping: I forget, therefore I am.

Crepuscular

Late in the afternoon the light
  at this tapering end
of Long Island not so much fails
  as filters out the sun,
and in a month amid stances
  restores the word twilight
to its original senses:
  the day between, or half
itself, as when Locke alluded
  to 'the twilight of probability.'

But if at this moment I see
  its application, still
the word comes hard, appalling me
  in poetry: it sounds
too much like toilet, and Verlaine
  becomes impossible
to translate, for instance, even
  when the real thing happens
around me, as at this moment.
  Should reality sound poetical?

I sit at the French window (why
  else worry about Verlaine?)
worrying too about Robert Frost
  who said either we write
out of a strong weakness (poets
  love oxymoronic forms)
for the Muse, or we write because
  it seems like a good idea
to write. As the day tapers off
  like the island, I wonder at my choice.

Indeed, have I chosen? Outside
        the open window, Max
the dog is staring in at me,
        I can still see him, pale
against the darkening lawn, now,
        for he is a white dog
that has just found out the difference
        between Inside and Outside,
the choice that always, when there is
        a door, even a French one, must be made.

Thresholds for Max have lately meant
        a problem: he lies across
the sill supposing, I suppose,
        he'll have the best of both —
whatever world looms on each side;
        why, as another French
romantic said, must a door be
        either open or shut?
Max whines if I go to the toilet
        and close him out — for him the word toilet

clearly suggests the twilight, some
        subliminal ending.
These French doors ajar (ah, Musset!)
        merely frustrate decision;
and as the moments modify
        each blade of grass, blossom,
bush and branch, suddenly showing,
        in a light committed
to impartiality, yet
        another aspect: the night side of things,

Max trots over to the window
        where I sit wondering
if I want to elope with her
        or just be good friends, more
like a brother to the Muse, and
        gravely—I guess it is
gravely, in fact I'll never know—
        shoves his white face against
the pane, nose flattened, of the door
        and barks at me for being inside it.

But if I join him on the lawn
        that is gray now, he will
only dash back to the table
        where I have been, and bark
at me out on the silver grass.
        The Muse indoors, or on
the road? Possessed, or befriended?
        Choice is impossible.
Robert Frost is impossible.
        Max and I know the truth, quite possibly,

that the light survives a long time
        here on Long Island as
elsewhere, and then will come to terms
        with darkness, and we call
the terms *evening,* our term for time
        when neither power has
dominion, the air balances,
        but just for now, and then
the odds are on the dark again.
        Max and I know this too: it will be night.

II

Intimations of Mortality

The case grows more interesting the more I get
to understand the man. He has certain qualities
very largely developed: selfishness, secrecy and
purpose. His redeeming quality is a love of ani-
mals, though, indeed, he has such curious turns
in it that I sometimes imagine he is only ab-
normally cruel.

—*From Dr. Seward's diary,*
in Dracula *by Bram Stoker*

i

This little boy I was
Collected other lives,
Saved them up to spoil: not gullible
Prey—goldfish in the brown lily pond
Or the old bulldog—no, he was out
After strange gods and not
Familiars. Look for him
Working his way down the privet hedge,
Clapping bees in a cyanide jar,
His grandmother's long darning needle
Sliding them by like beads
Until he is garlanded with a lei
Of gored furies dying on the thread.
Or find him, tomorrow, playing house
Underneath that same murmuring hedge,
When a fieldmouse almost
Runs right into his hands:
An hour's "play" is enough to make out
Of what had once been so prompt and smooth

An emblem of mouse *accidie,*
    Stupefied in his hand,
Torpid and blotchy, plainly without
Energy even to squeal or bite.
He would have to kill it: half-filled
A milk bottle, pushed the thing down in.
    It would not drown, crawling
    Up, falling back, silent,
Sad and strangely obstinate, until
He panicked, dropped the bottle, ran off
Terrified for months of some coming
    Vengeance in empty lots.

ii

    The Mouse God pursues
Me no longer, and hearing no harsh
Voices from the grass I guess the Bee
People have relented. I am free.
Today there is no more such saving up,
    Lives inevitably
    Having come to mean deaths.
I shall not be hunting any more,
But wear a string of failures, love,
Hanging stingless round my neck.
    Last night, when I returned
    From what I call real life
To you, the years lying between us
Like a hedge (the flowers fallen now),
Both of us stalled in your empty house,
The coffee as cold as the comfort,
    I saw for once, at least,
    As in a twinge of pain,
The sense of my old animal plunders:

How else do we know what we are,
Save by tokens of what we have ruined?
    How else read right the signs
Of our surrender to ourselves, save
In terms of what we are scared to save?
We mourned the time we had lost, chances
You could not keep, I could not let go.
    And I saw the future
    Impaled on its cruel coils,
A murdered mouse sliding down the glass.

Private Drive: Memorial for a
Childhood Playmate

i

Trying to keep out of the builders' way, we
trampled the strawberries that grew wild
and cut our fingers on red
tiles where the blood might
not show so
much.
The mud was like the Argonne trenches (pictures
we giggled over, atrocities
in the library where we
sneaked cokes and candy,
forbidden
luxe!) —
when the men went home we bled and licked our wounds
as we watched them go. There would
be something new in
this muddy field:
it was that
spring
they were building a studio with glass brick
for walls, and as we played underneath
the scaffolding you told me:
— I'm going to go
away now
so
don't be surprised to see her when she comes back.
— Who's *she,* Lois, who's coming back here?
You just smiled crooked, saying
in your grownup voice:
— Another
girl,

dressed so much like me and looking so like me
you wouldn't know it wasn't me, but
there is a way to tell, you
said, one way you'll know
I'm someone
else.
—How, Lois, how can I tell it won't be you?
—This girl, you said, will be speaking French.
—What'll I say back?—Just say
Bonjour, Mademoiselle,
and then you
ran
around the glass-brick corner (for that was when
Modern meant having corner windows)
of your father's studio,
or mother's, maybe—
it's hers now.
I
waited, sucking my thumb, incredulous but
longing for you to come back. And O
you did, but who knew how well
things would be arranged?
You *have* been
changed!
But so have I, I'm changed too, I'm you now and
everything I know of you is me:
today *I* speak French, there's been
another war, *we* do
not speak, we
spoil.

Palermo's Landscape Garden lay
South of the city
On a rock foundation—shales perforated
By intrusive gneiss, limestone caves
And lintels crannied
In soil that made an easy work of wonders:
Sudden glimpses into a Gulph,
Tunnels of baroque
Surprise from which the prospect dropt, out of sight,
To earth no more than a few feet
Below. Here we came
At springtime for annuals and in the dead
Of winter our Christmas trees
(Roots balled, re-planted
Once the tinsel, still clinging, had served its turn).
Each season, whether obelisks
Were cumbered with snow
Or yellow with the lichen-scale that lingered
In the sandstone pores, each visit,
Lois would escape
The car, our calls, and as if she had been lured
Past the terraced tubs of lemon
By the beckoning
Statuary, would dash headlong to vanish
Into the phony labyrinth
Where cypresses, black
In December, leaned together, revealing
As I ran toward the place, only
Gray mortuary
Arches, silhouetted high and hopelessly,
Which by a tweak of perspective
All at once betrayed

(Absurdly tiny) from the path that circled
Above them, the secret old Nick
Palermo had learned
Probably from the Greek stones in Sicily:
Nothing has a size of its own.
I never found her,
Lois my suburban Proserpine, summoned
By what mystery, what message
In those rusty rocks,
Until she was ready to appear: standing
In pure importance at the end
Of a corridor,
The sun braiding shadows into her bright hair,
Or almost hidden, shivering
Where she had waited
In a shell of dim ivy, gone to earth — gone
For good now, as then in a game,
With all the rigor
Fun has to have: I found you, Lois,
Just where you left me, impatient
To be discovered
As you had been to get away from us all
Into a world of disciplined
Water, distinguished
Women, even if they were only concrete
And cracked more often than not.
The landscape garden
You hide in now is pretty nearly the same
As Palermo's commercial grot,
Annuals replaced
With Everlasting Care, evergreens set out
The way we used to do, but you
Not — you never, you
Nowhere, now, save in that past I don't suffer

But create, in a ritual
Precious to me for
Its banality. Nobody will be there
To see you in your bush of hair
Dance burning away,
But to me you will come, I will make you come,
Your face saturated in sleep
And nothing else left
In the landscape garden these late days of ours
But darkness, Lois, and disgrace.

iii

The Pierce-Arrow I took to be
self-illustrative,
like stickpins, almost winged its way; we
had started for the docks, at last
the *trip* had started!
First the circuit Olmsted had laid out,
Gothic rockeries — not Central
but Edgewater Park,
the same system of brick tunnels, vines
curtaining the mouths we roared
into, hissed along,
then out into sunlight. Past the Great
Lakes Fairground to the Flats
where sulfur, mounded
in yellow cones like frozen custard,
waited for the mills. *We* waited
for the light to change:
Lois, Gramma, the chauffeur and I,
heading downtown to the Old Pier
where we would embark,
limousine and all, on the night boat

for the Cape. Lois sat with Gramma
and the French bulldog
Bootsie, I was beside the chauffeur
as the ponderous car crept up
the gangway. "You can
drive right on!" I marvelled, Lois knew
that all along, or said she did,
Bootsie barked a lot
when we got to our cabin, and Fred,
the chauffeur, disappeared into
part of the ferry
that was fit for chauffeurs. Shuddering
already, the black ship slid off
after a sharp blast,
and we were away! The light had changed.

The smell of apple peels, all
in one scarlet worm
my Gramma could slice off not looking,
filled the cabin where we lay
in bed together,
"No harm," she told your mother, "at nine:
they're only children still." Still,
waiting for the light
to be put out in the apple-sweet air,
I knew what I would do, what
you were with me for
in that upper berth. Once her snoring
started, part of the steamer
machinery now,
I unbuttoned to your bones and rib
by rib explored your body
captive in my arms.
Gramma found us, saw no harm in what

she saw by the morning light:
two children tangled
in each other's hair, mostly naked
but only nine, and the boat
was nearly anchored.
Fred was there, ready with the car, and
Bootsie was more than ready.
There was still a day's
drive, and Gramma wanted to arrive
before the light turned, the sea
went dark on the rocks.
Lois and Gramma shared a birthday:
that was the treat—this whole trip
would be a birthday
present, imagine! Gramma explained,
giving someone the seashore
just for being born.

Gramma this year would be a hundred
and in my child's eye always
was. Lois took space
on a black ship to hell, and I lost
them both. Gramma taught me how
to peel an apple,
how to remember, how to reach back.
Lois wanted only to get
safe ashore, to get
out of the stream of our animal
perpetuations. If only
I can keep in one
cabin the smell of apples and some
part of that hunger to know:
then let the light turn
bad, I will be *both* in the darkness

they left me, I won't take sides . . .
　　　The sea was brilliant
on the rocks my Gramma called Squeakers,
　　　and there seemed to be plenty
　　　　　of time. Lois must
have forgotten about the night boat,
　　　I decided, nothing was wrong
　　　　　anyway—I knew
more, that was all the difference it made.
　　　We went down to the beach where
　　　　　the tide had left signs
for Bootsie, not even unpacking
　　　first: Lois and I undressed
　　　　　in front of Gramma
and Fred, then the tide pools took us.
　　　Thrashing back, wrong to the light,
　　　　　Lois surged against me
and exclaimed as the shadows ran down
　　　to the water's edge, "Look, look,
　　　　　how it keeps changing!"

TEAR-SHEETS

*

There was a cave under the piano
Where we could live, the animals left us
Alone there, and in the dark place behind
The pedal harp you told me you had learned
How we could have children too, whole litters
Of them if we liked! I would have to pull
Down my corduroy knickers and you would hike
Up your dress, and when our cold buttocks touched
Then they would come, the children. They have gone.

**

You hooked your legs over the crooked branch,
Your face on a level with mine, smiling,
Reversed, into my eyes as you hung there
And took great bites around your apple,
I can still hear the sound of your small teeth
Breaking the skin. There were apples all
Over the tree, and on the ground under
You as you swayed from your knobby knees. "Look!"
You cried, "I'm swallowing *up!*" Swallowed up.

***

At our progressive musicale, we danced
The Planets, I was Uranus of course
And you were one of my moons. Revolving
Until we were dizzy in our orbits
We stumbled across the gymnasium,
And our fond audience applauded us.
Across the black sky the great Figures go,
Each with its set of moons regularly
Appearing and occulted. One went out.

****

You led me into the dark kitchen where
The Monitor-top ticked and warned. Nighttime
Made the shelves creak, and the enamel chairs
Arched their backs like companionable ghosts
Of cats. I was thirsty. Gradually
In the dark, a glass was made to exist
By the white milk you poured into it. All
I could see of the invisible form
Was the ascending level. Spilled milk now.

I hid behind the dying clubhouse oak
    Until my mother signalled,
Then I ran down. Lois, our big houses
Loomed above the bunkers, your new glass brick
    Blinking like a semaphor;
Mother drove, I watched the ball go by me
And the fairway led right into the trap.
    "For catching little boys?"
I asked her: was that why I was not allowed?
Words alarmed me: *course* sounded bland enough
    If ambiguous, but *links*
Meant only chains, and even the red flags
Could not make up for *traps* and *holes*
    And worst of them all, *the rough.*
I kept my distance from the olive-skinned
Sicilian caddies, so little older
    Than I was then, but living
Already in an enclave of intent
I had not ventured into yet. But when
    I did, they would still be there.

Minnows made the creeks murmur, a black dog
    I was forbidden to pet
Ran out behind me and despoiled the ninth.
But here the fauna mostly seemed to fail
    Just where it might flourish best
In this slip-cover geology: what
Bright and heraldic beasts inhabited
    These baby Himalayas,
Giant lawns, what creatures haunted these groves
Of German-silver birch? The *genius*
    Loci seemed to be a harrow,

And a constant drone of machines drowned out
The birds. It was a backward country, Lo,
    That beckoned to your gamey
And not quite inconsolable nights. All
At once the stories spread, a greenskeeper
    On his rounds had found you out
There with Mario, furious to see
The grounds were used for hunting after all.

    Somehow we had failed you, whom
My golfing mother called your "natural
Acquaintances," and from the guardians
    Of our games, pool boys, caddies,
Even the leathery tennis pro, you learned
A lesson that lay in wait for you, Lo,
    Waiting on the tee for lays:
What we do blurs over what we did before.
If landscape is moralized, then the course
    Addresses us both, myself
Forbidden, you a later trespasser.
I see what is linked together now, and
    What is lost. Was it the same
Thing that kept me lurking behind the oak,
Lois, while you larked out on the cold grass?
    We were the honest sportsmen
Obeying different rules for the same game,
Only I am playing still—you ended
    Black-faced on the garage floor,
The car motor running like a mower.

Further Instructions to the Architect

Now about the attic: please allow
    For easy access to the roof
So Cousin Agnes can get out there.
    Fall, did you say? Remember all
    The servants' bedrooms must include
,A dream book in the dresser, and there was
    Always a gate across the stairs:
Our pantry sibyl walked in her sleep,
    Read tea leaves, knew what "horses" meant.

    Make sure the smell of apple peel
    Lingers in the master bedroom,
Keep lewd prints for the *Decameron*
Locked in the library, and repair
    The stained glass over the landing:
If the Lorelei's hair is still clear
The amber can always be replaced.
    I hear one ilex has fallen
Across the pond. Better plant rushes
    So the frogs will come back, evenings,
And sing their songs; restore the *allée*
Of Lombardy poplars where the doves
    Nested: we need all our mourners.

    See that the four black junipers
Don't overgrow the lawn: after dark
    The silver grass is luminous
Around them. There should be a wheezing
French bulldog on my grandmother's lap,
    Of course, and the sound of grape seeds
    Being flicked onto the porch floor
Where Ernestine is reading. Even

The corridor back to whatever
    Surprise you have in store must be
Merely the one between the (witch's)
    Kitchen and the dim hall closet
Where velveteen hangers may have turned
By now to something else unlikely.

You can't help getting it right if you
    Listen to me. Recognition
Is not to be suppressed. Why the whole
Place seems just the way it was, I tell you
    I was there last night: in dreams
We are always under house arrest.

III

Bonnard: A Novel

The tea party at Le Cannet. Just as we arrived it began,
                a downpour, and kept on.
                This might have been the time
before: Charles-Xavier playing Scriabin etudes, all the others
                at the open window.
                A landscape—lawn, garden,
strawberry patch, Japanese footbridge, barges moving on the river
                beyond—as in Verlaine
                behind a mist of rain,
and the regular noise of the rain on tens of thousands of leaves:
                such is the prose that wears
                the poem's guise at last.
White cats, one in almost every chair, pretend not to be watching
                young Jean worry the dog.
                Sophie, damp, dashes in
dishevelled from the forest, dumping out a great bag of morels
                on the table: the white
                cloth will surely be spoiled,
but the mushrooms look iridescent, like newly opened oysters
                in the raindark air, blue
                by this light. Calling it
accidental is only declaring that it exists. Then tea
                downstairs, Jean opening
                the round pantry window:
the smell of wet soil and strawberries with our cinnamon toast: all
                perception is a kind
                of sorting out, one green
from another, parting leaf from leaf, but in the afternoon rain
                signs and shadows only,

the separate life renounced,
until that resignation comes, in which all selfhood surrenders . . .
Upstairs, more Scriabin
and the perfect gestures
of Sophie and Jean playing ball with the dog. All the cats are deaf.
Steady rain. The music
continues, Charles-Xavier
shouting over the notes, ignoring them: "Beatitude teaches
nothing. To live without
happiness and not wither—
there is an occupation, almost a profession." Take the trees:
we could "contrive to do
without trees," but not leaves,
Charles-Xavier explains from the piano, still playing, "we require
their decorum that is
one of congestion, till
like Shelley we become lewd vegetarians." Apprehensive
about the rain, I ask
Jean to order a closed
carriage for Simone. The doctor frowns—a regular visitor
these days?—and frightens her,
eyeing Sophie's mushrooms;
his diagnosis: toadstools. Scriabin diminishes. Is the dog
lost? Jean rushes outside.
Punishment of the dog:
he is forbidden the strawberry patch. Darker now. One candle
is found for the piano,
and the music resumes
with Debussy, a little sphere of yellow in the sopping dusk.
The river's surface looks—
is it the rain?—like the sea
in shallows: this moment is an instance of the world becoming
a mere convenience,
more or less credible,

and the old questions rise to our lips—but have we spoken a word?—
           before we remember,
           prompted by the weather
probably, or the time of day, that we already know something:
           we are not newborn, then.
           What is it that we know?
The carriage comes at last, but it is an open carriage, merely
           hooded. We crowd under,
           fending off the last drops
with a violet golf umbrella Charles-Xavier has somehow
           managed for us. A slow
           cold drive under the trees,
Simone balancing the suspect mushrooms in her lap. I tell her
           it is not dangerous:
           we cannot die, but are
in this light or lack of it—trees dripping, the sky fraudulent—
           much less individuals
           than we hope or fear to be.
Once home, we shall have a little supper of Sophie's fresh-picked morels.

Ossorio Assembles a Universe

You had things enough there to make anyone
        uneasy, I'm not denying that.
The glass eyes alone, or in pairs, reminding
        me of the more unsightly spare parts
cluttering up the slabs in Count Frankenstein's
        ancestral lab . . . The antelope horns,
eland, elk, whatever forked or pronged itself
        into offence, waited in rows for
you to saw them down. Sorted into sizes,
        driftwood littered the beaches of your
intent, along with fur buttons, spurious
        pre-Columbian heads, coq feathers
prepared for another Dietrich revival,
        and it was all to serve something else:

Your Will. Other visitors I know were spooked
        by what Auden calls, in our landscape,
the heterogeneous *dreck* you handled
        so deftly as you steered them around
archipelagos of coral, mulberry
        roots and broken mirrors, readily
avoiding whales' teeth in tarpits of plastic
        which had not yet dried. Who first devised
the nervous gag—that we could shortly expect,
        given the rate you were going now,
to see Someone we knew laid out at length here
        from fontanel to pelvic girdle?

So sinister to some your good manners seemed,
    I suppose and, craven, shuddered too.

More accurately, that courtliness of yours,
    the grand seigneurial style no one
of us felt he quite deserved, suggests
    another circle, another sphere—
when callers were shown the Grand Duke's collection
    of coelanaglyphic intaglios,
carnelian seals and Tanagra figurines
    by Councillor von Goethe himself,
who took a curious pleasure, Weimar found,
    in fingering such antiquities.
Appropriate that like Goethe too, you worked
    in an untenanted theater,
commanding your queer creations from the stage
    while we sidled past them on the floor.

For what dismayed us here was no more the smell
    of narwhal tusks macerating than
the sight of seven hundred Cuban tree snails,
    each in its rhinestone socket. What we
quailed at, queasily, was the real heresy
    in these concoctions. God knows you had
given the Fathers every chance, there were still
    Crosses all over the place—chiefly
carved out of treated feces, of course—but not
    even the Church could express for you
the True Cross between what is worth redeeming
    in us and what we are. You would do
that yourself. No wonder if we winced to see
    Mephisto smiling at his wild forge!

Do It Again:
Didactic Stanzas

i   Being! Being! the body rants
    When pain is the color of certain events:
        Surely it's better to scream "I suffer"
        Than say "This landscape is ugly."

ii   Comes a time, in the dead of doubt,
    When action alone is certainty:
        The heart's still-lifes are still
        Only after a violent death.

iii   Pale in the prospect of my love
    Your body lies, a fiction but
        My one chance of saving what
        Time and society erode.

iv   So I return to the gestures of lust
    As if it were to innocence:
        Repetition is the only mode
        That nature knows of memory.

A Speaking Likeness

A lady I knew died not long ago,
    having lately passed
her eighty-seventh year on the planet.
    She had been, they said,
the image of Aunt Emily, and that
    was her surest self,
she explained—a "dead ringer" all her life.

Some years before the end, I remember,
    she defined the phrase
which had to do with horses, fraudulent
    entries in a race,
false names for better odds. That is no sense
    I care to keep, for
Emily's niece was, though equine, genuine

enough despite bewildering contrasts:
    her long bony face
had its abrupt square black brows affording
    the authority
of constraint under cotton-wool hair
    recalled to order
by the cabaline, arched New England nose—

every feature *told,* most the wrinkled mouth
    that told me once—last
probably of all the times the story
    was insisted on—
what afternoons were like in Amherst, days
    when she entertained
the posthumously famous Emily.

"You could say I knew her by ear. She spoke
        to me from the hall
while I sat—age nine—as I was told, not
        looking round to see
my 'peculiar' aunt who would not appear,
        playing my pieces
for her on the sable Chickering grand.

But glimpsed her when I came in, impassive
        as porcelain, hands
folded in her lap, eyes fixed straight ahead.
        She liked Mendelssohn,
would often command, her voice cracked but loud
        enough to carry
over the stylish *presto,* 'try again.'

Not that I blundered so often, the notes
        were nimble in fact,
but for her, trying must have been the word
        for any doing.
Sometimes I think she slid away: I saw
        the window darken
and a long shadow move across the lawn.

I played on, though, in the dim house while she
        obliterated
her life in that secret way she had learned.
        We only learned it
when my mother found them in the attic—
        sewn in neat packets,
all that was left: eighteen hundred poems."

Such was the old lady's story, who became
        soon after, a dead

ringer of the other sort, not having
        Emily's "success
in circuit." The odds were against her. *Wrecked,*
        solitary, here,
the old niece faltered—foundered, like us all

on consternation's carrousel. Poets, farewell
        and goodnight, ladies!
Earth itself must turn to a dead ringer
        in time, speeding round
its unavailing sun. "Circumference
        is my business,"
Emily consoled, an old maid cherishing

the world in her image—all men nieces
        of an absconded
Progenitor (*Burglar, Banker, Father!*)—
        and only concerned
with what she felt could surround. Yet scorned
        the fond foolishness
which every morning "prayed to an Eclipse."

"The mind of the heart must live," she declared,
        more confident with
no doctrine but the bundles left upstairs
        than her dying niece,
like us, could afford to be. There's reason
        we have lost our trust
in the mind as in the heart. *Why* must it live?

The old woman I knew died, the image of
        Emily. Poems
return to the attic or remain there.
        And as the mind rings

its unacknowledged spoil like Gemini,
    the best we can do
is recognize faces, find resemblances.

For Hephaistos, with Reference
to the Deaths in a Dry Year
of Cocteau, Roethke and MacNeice

Whatever I may mean could not be equally
well conveyed by gestures but can be expressed,
if at all, in speech (that is why I wish to write
this poem), and wherever speech is necessary,
lying and self-deception are both possible.
        —W. H. Auden

I come on down the common street, a smear
Of stores like neon sores, where citizens
Whose needs and greeds will never overlap
Are busy buying up their brainless haul
In a Season reasonable merchants fear
Will be far too slack for a rainless fall
(Waiters will give you no water today
Until you tell them to), but painless all
The same for a pining time of the year.

Beside me slides the shadow of my love,
Or the body which cast that shadow once
And darkens my discernment ever since,
And now our shadows, unobserved, remove
Themselves along the pavement, past the place
Where G-men have raided a restaurant
For serving water, past the movie house,
The bar, the bank, and just as we confront
The bookshop you come out: we're face to face.

In a year when the poets are dying
Of madness not murrains, not rot but rage,
And only Great Statesmen live to great age,
When we mourn a forger who died trying
To lock both profiles into the one face

(Only he looked too many ways), and mourn
Our crazy countryman who gave his voice
To the high wind that howled him down, and scorned
All synonyms but violence for grace;

In a year when your Iceland playmate died,
Leaving not much more than a thirties' drawl
And your collaboration, it is all
The more reassuring to find your head
Suddenly bobbing up, surprised, beside
My own in that place, your sane face showing,
By the way it was wrinkled, all that had
Happened outside you, a way of knowing
The Good, more than a way of going bad—

A letter to the future that your life
Had found much crumpled underneath some chair
And hastily smoothed out: I looked, and there
Was no profession in your look back save
A final harmlessness that made it clear
You could not be a bum, despite your air
Of tweedy degeneration. The stare
Exchanged was all that passed between for proof
I knew you, even as my onetime love.

Wondering, I forgot my words and lost
All presence of mind as you labored past.
And yet you taught me, taught us all a way
To speak our minds, and only now, at last
Free of you, my old ventriloquist,
Have I suspected what I have to say
Without hearing you say it for me first.
Like my old love, I have survived you best
By leaving you, and so you're here to stay.

In a thirsty season, then, while we wait
For all the upstate reservoirs to fill,
In a year whose characteristic stamp
Will probably be the admission of "camp"
Into the Unabridged, what better style
Of thanking you for your too-famous state
Of being here, the indescribable
Dasein of this moment—you like a tramp,
My lorn love, the long drouth—than keeping still?

"Even the Most Beautiful
Sunset Is Boring in
Three-Quarters of an Hour"

We sat on the deck
of a celebrated decorator
    as the sun declined
and fell to its customary ruin.

    "A little applause,"
you drawled, as it finally disappeared,
    "might bring it back up,
seeing how well-rehearsed the performance was."

    "Recapitulate—
I dare you—the progress of French landscape,"
    our host exulted,
"from Boudin to Bonnard faster than *that!*"

    certain that the sun
had been trained in the greatest ateliers
    to gain such *maîtrise*
where all of Europe's scholars drew—a blank.

    "Or else, I should say,"
I said, "the sun had seen far too many
    Japanese movies
for its own good as a cameraman."

    You laughed at us both
and reported how as a girl in Holland
    you watched the sun fade
from the terrace, over the flat red fields,

and then ran upstairs
to see it vanish all over again.
   "Which was, I suppose,"
you ended, "what is known as a Dutch treat."

   Our host reminded
us about Goethe's put-down of sunsets . . .
   Besides, it was dark.
Soon we went indoors and turned on some lights.

Oystering

"Messieurs, l'huitre étoit bonne. Adieu. Vivez
en paix."
— *Boileau*

Secret they are, sealed, annealed, and brainless
And solitary as Dickens said, but
They have something to say: that there is more
Than one way to yield. The first—and the hardest,
The most nearly hindered—is when you pull
Them off the rocks, a stinking, sawing sedge
Sucking them back under the black mud, full
Of hermit crabs and their borrowed snailshells,
Minnows scattering like superstitions,
The surf dragging, and every power
Life permits them holding out, holding on
For dear life. Sometimes the stones give way first,
Before *they* will, but still we gather them,
Even if our hands are bloody as meat,
For a lunch Queen Victoria preferred:
"A barrel of Wellfleet oysters, points down"
Could last across the ocean, all the way
To Windsor, wakening a widow's taste.
We ate them this afternoon, out of their
Armor that was formidably grooved, though
It proved our own reversal wiser still:
Keep the bones and stones inside, or never
Leave the sea. "He was a brave man," Swift said,
"Who first eat one." Even now, precedent
Of centuries is not always enough.
Driving the knife into muscles that mould
The valves so close to being impartial,
Surrender, when it comes—and it must come:

Lavish after that first grudging release
Back there in the sea, the giving over
Of despair, this time—makes me speculate.
Like Oscar and oysters, I feel "always
Slightly immortal when in the sea": what
Happens now we are out? Is the risk worth
While for a potential pearl? No, what we're
Really after is the moment of release,
The turn and tear of the blade that tightens,
Tortures, ultimately tells. When you spread
The shells, something always sticks to the wrong
One, and a few drops of liquor dribble
Into the sand. Scrape it off: in the full
Half, as well as a Fautrier, a Zen
Garden, and the smell of herring brine that
Ferenczi said we remember from the womb,
Lunch is served, in shiny stoneware sockets,
Blue milk in the sea's filthiest cup. More
Easily an emblem for the inner man
Than dinner, sundered, for the stomach. We
Take them queasily, wonder as we gulp
When it is—then, now, tomorrow—they're dead.

The Author of 'Christine'

For Sanford Friedman

Often waking
before the sun decreed the kind of day
                    this one would be
            or by its absence left
            the verdict up to him,
he gazed in doubt
at the blank slate and wondered, blue or gray,
                    what *he* might leave
            scribbled against the time
            the darkness came for good;
that was his text.
The trouble was, he realized, to choose.
                    He roused the rooms,
            walking around the house
            that had to share the day
with his despair,
raising each blind as if it were the dead,
                    the morning light
            a record of his progress
            in sudden shafts of dust.
The trouble was
in trying so: imagining Christine
                    to be this way
            or that. Reality
            had to be happened on,
one had to *find*,
not create it. There is always life itself
                    beyond the prose
            that declares it to us,
            life being an absolute

134

we aspire to,
bliss, but surely cannot reach. Today
                    he would write more,
              creating in Christine
              his hopes of what was real,
knowing 'the real'
by what becomes of it and of ourselves.
                    Dust was his proof:
              the life we know we live
              is simply not enough:
the work dissolves,
leaches into the medium and is lost
                    there like water;
              the words sink into sand,
              dust dances in the sun.
Christine was chaos,
parcels of his own childhood where the past
                    appeared to be
              no more than behavior,
              merely authority.
Take the big scene
when Giorgio, leaving the attic, hobbles down
                    and asks Christine
              about the box, she pales
              and follows him back—why?
"The novelist
seldom penetrates character, the mystery
                    remains intact."
              Thank you Thomas Hardy,
              sighing over the mess
you made for her
yet asking "Where was Tess's guardian angel *then?*"
                    He much preferred
              Hardy the poet now,

                    that doubting Thomas who
when Swinburne died
declared him "the sweet rival of the waves
                    and once their peer
                in sad improvisations."
                That was character.
To make Christine
out of what was not his choice, participate
                    in what would change
                her, like the waves, and him . . .
                Shoving his desk outside
into the sun,
he decided *Christine* could not be written from
                    his waking hopes:
                by will to set himself
                or the reader apart
from what the world
might be without the waves, bereft of wet
                    and wilderness.
                No, he would have to let
                the weeds of wavering
flourish, rehearse
to both of them, the reader and himself,
                    not ways that help
                us on but that will help
                acknowledge our defeat
in getting on —
that would be *Christine,* his novel, and
                    Christine be him.

An Old Dancer

Because there is only one of you in all of time
. . . the world will not have it . . .
                              — *Martha Graham*

Your props had always been important:
Preposterous poniards, rings and thorns,
Things without a name you fell upon
Or through. Now they are your props indeed.
Take that iron prong you dangle from,
Strung up, slung like a sick animal
Who used to rise as straight as any tree
Without such corporal irony.

Propped then, you make no bones, or only
Bones, of husbanding your strength. For strength
Was your husband, and you're widowed now.
The face that was a mask of wonder
Wizens into the meaninglessness
Of some Osaka marionette,
And there is properly little more
That you can do for us than think.

What thoughts are yours, or were yours when
Half-visionary and half-voyeur
You tore the veils from Remembered Women,
Rarely lovely, except as the space
That took them into its hugest mouth
Makes any movement lovely: at first
It was enough for you to be them,
Violent, often vague as they come,

Until the years and the work of years
Led you beyond being into more
Than self supplied: now you must review
What you have been and let the others
Do. What you were a whole theater
Has become. What have you lost by that
Exchange, save as the tree loses by
Giving up its leaves and standing bare?

O Dancer, you have lost everything,
Shuddering on your iron gallows-tree.
Bane, bone and violence, you answer
Yeats in kind, unkindest witch of all:
"We know the dancer from the dance" by age,
By growing old. The dance goes on,
The dancers go, and you hang here
Like stale meat on your dead steel branch.

The Encounter

The landscape—at least what you can see of it,
      for these are contours that afford
   no rest, no recompense after a long
stare, the very air drinks down the scenery,
      all but a yellow scum the sun
   .deposits round the bottom of the glass—
the landscape is the color *lion,* the low
      hills like a ring of lions then.
    The light leaves nothing upright in your mind.
There are no birds. Noon, it must be always noon,
      the way your shadow dribbles out
   into the sand: if the sun were modest
would it be the sun? And you have been walking
      toward those same mountains forever.
    Have they changed at all? Is there even one
tree to tell by? Whatever lies between you
      and the edge of existence
   makes no sign. There is the desert and there
is the sky: daylight is the way things behave.
      The ridges of pale sand, in rows,
   parody oceans, and just as you climb
over the next one you see something shipwrecked—
      ribs of a boat that has been starved
   to death? As you approach, the boat dissolves
into a Being like a giant insect,
      spider? spider-crab? What is it, sprawled
   on a stretch of Nowhere that somehow leads
your mind back to the other Thebes? Whatever
      waits there, motionless, is ready
   to take you on, turning into itself
as you come, until you learn. Surely it is
      Egyptian enough to find her

here (for you see *her* now), isolated
as much as you are, but all the same at home.
        She has the posture of lions,
    and closing in on her you recognize
what first had fooled you into superstition:
        the spidery legs are simply
    articulated rods attached to what
appears a diving board, where the insolent
        fringe of red-beaded tassels hangs
    swaying even in this exhausted air,
eight feet up, or twelve—in the heat, everything
        looks bigger, distances deceive,
    your memory stops meaning anything.
All that matters is the ring of ragged hills
        behind you and ahead of you
        which suddenly funnel down to her. Her,
up there on a plush platform whose silver legs
        thrust like crooked telescopes
    into the sand. You seem to hesitate
a second, then swing the sweaty leather cloak
        down from one shoulder and drop it
    hissing as it subsides behind your heels.
Now you go straight up to her, not hurrying
        but not holding back either,
    until you stand just where the platform casts
a tiny oblong of shadow. Nothing moves.
        She hunches above you, arms flat,
    and you can see her nails over the rim:
they are silver too. You grab the rope ladder—
        what else is there to do? You look
    up once, look back, and then begin to climb . . .
The ladder shifts with your weight, all the ropes creak
        helplessly, rung by rung, until
    your head appears above the silly fringe.

"It's a little girl, that's all she is, a child!"
        startled, as your eyes come level
        with her hard breasts, you think, "This won't take long."
But then, slinging one leg up, you discover
        what you had to see to believe:
        the need in her expectant loins, betrayed
by a tremor that seems to dim the bright hair
        sprouting like wheat across her hips
        (all your ideas about children change).
The girl lies still, still peering without alarm
        over her intricate shoulder
        as your other leg clears the tassels now:
you are beside her. As if her body yawned,
        she celebrates your being here
        by rolling over lazily, lightly,
looming above you like a lioness then
        and lays one talon on your chest.
    You let your eyes travel the distance up
her arms to where her face hangs toward you, clustered
        just above the beginner's breasts
        too firm to be pendulous; you fondle them
a while and trail one hand along her belly
        to where the long thighs arch over
        your own. She is an animal on you,
a smooth beast grateful for the rough appetite
        within her—how the gratitude
        rages in her exultant flesh, even
to yours! Naked and lovely, the muscles slide,
        then tighten till she is standing,
        warm feet against your rib cage, and you gaze
up the gold columns, past the foreshortened fleece,
        the minor breasts, to where she smiles.
    You loved her on all fours, you love
her standing more, the way we love the naked

always: it is ourselves we love.
The memory awakens, you recall
what you can do with yourself. And first of all
you can perpetuate yourself:
your hands slide up her parted thighs as if
on pulleys, her knees perform, and suddenly
she is down, and only one thing
stands now, ready as your senseless senses
let you know that she is ready too. Impaled
abruptly on the prong of flesh
she writhes, yet you do not move, it is her
moving that sends the answer deeper in, still
deeper, till with a scream she knows
you know. But had there been a question? When
was it put—when the pale animal topped you,
or when the woman made you praise
her where she stood, or when between your legs
you pinned her like a thrush upon a thorn: man.
Nothing is hard now, all the rage
that called you into question dies down to
something poor, exhausted, and a little cold.
The animal sighs, and her breath
goes sour. Forgetting where you are, you push
away the fishy thing, and with a sucking sound
her suddenly gray belly rolls off,
rolls over again, until her legs catch
in the ladder. Down spills her body, knees hooked,
hair reaching almost to the sand,
and if you will descend at all you must
employ the ladder of her limbs. You do it,
retching every time your hand
skids on the oily hide . . . You touch the ground
ahead of your shadow, stand a moment more
there where she dangles to a halt.

The sun has not shifted, yet from somewhere
in an altered sky you hear a terrible
        chord, a crash as of thunder but
    shrieking too, as you reach out and shove her,
just once, to see what she will do. Not a thing.
        "Little girls!" you think, dismissing
    what had almost been a doubt, "the next time
let it be a woman ripe enough to last."
        You lean over, pick up your cloak
    and for all the folly of the sun, spread
it on your shoulders, starting up the long grade
        easily to where you must go.
    The sand gives like a skin under your soles.
Do you look back once? Yes, once, to discover
        that the insect you had supposed
    you saw is there again: down in the pit
out of which you are toiling now, an ant lion
        attends. You are almost too far,
    in another minute or so, to tell
what hangs down from it. Again there is no more
        than a bug behind you, nothing
    more. The ring of dirty hills reappears
at closer range. A bird materializes
        out of nowhere, somehow, singing
    and you know you must be nearer to Thebes
than all the leagues of empty sand can show. Like
        a hero, you are on your way.